Schools of Hope

How Julius Rosenwald Helped Change African American Education

Norman H. Finkelstein

CALKINS CREEK
AN IMPRINT OF HIGHLIGHTS
Honesdale, Pennsylvania

Text copyright © 2014 by Norman H. Finkelstein
All rights reserved

For information about permission to reproduce selections from this book,
please contact permissions@highlights.com.

Calkins Creek
An Imprint of Highlights
815 Church Street
Honesdale, Pennsylvania 18431
Printed in China

ISBN: 978-1-59078-841-7

Library of Congress Control Number: 2013951346

First edition
10 9 8 7 6 5 4 3 2 1

Designed by Tim Gillner
Production by Margaret Mosomillo
Titles set in Aachen Bold
Text set in Adobe Jenson

For Illy,
Iliana Liora Sugarman

Various terms (*Negro, black,* and *colored*) identify African Americans in this book according to the time period and the documents and quotations in which the words appear.

Built in 1923, the new Gloucester County Training School in Virginia (background), with its bright classrooms, replaced the old school (inset) that was in poor condition.

Julius Rosenwald established the fund that bore his name. Its greatest accomplishment was the building of more than 5,300 schools for African American children in the South during the first decades of the twentieth century.

Foreword

Give While You Live.

—Julius Rosenwald's philosophy

My grandfather was Julius Rosenwald, and he was a truly remarkable man. Unfortunately, I never knew him. He died ten years before I was born. But I researched and wrote his biography and discovered the grandfather I never knew.

In the early 1900s, under his leadership, Sears, Roebuck and Company became the largest retail establishment in the world. Rosenwald's office door was always open, and any employee could come to see him. According to a 1917 *Forbes* magazine article, Rosenwald was leaving the huge Sears, Roebuck plant on the West Side of Chicago one day with a friend. It was quitting time, and thousands of employees were on their way home. The friend turned to the Sears president and asked, "How does it feel, Mr. Rosenwald, to have so many people working for you?" "Why, I never think of it in that way," he replied. "I always think of them as just working with me."

Because of the success of Sears, Roebuck, Julius Rosenwald became a wealthy man. From a relatively young age, he had started giving money to charitable causes.

At first, he contributed money mostly to Jewish causes, but he soon branched out. In 1917, Rosenwald established his own foundation, the Julius Rosenwald Fund, which became one of the largest foundations of its day. Yet Rosenwald also imposed a novel restriction on the fund: he wanted the foundation to spend itself out of existence after his death. He believed that foundations that lasted forever made no sense because one could not predict what issues would be important five hundred years in the future. Moreover, he strongly believed that each generation should give money to the causes that it believed in. Rosenwald tried to interest some of his wealthy contemporaries to follow his example, but none were very interested.

Perhaps in no way was Julius Rosenwald more ahead of his time than in the matter of race. After meeting Booker T. Washington, Rosenwald became increasingly convinced that blacks and whites were equal and should be treated as such. As this book makes clear, Julius Rosenwald's most enduring legacy was the establishment of quality schools for African Americans. More than 5,300 were built in fifteen Southern states, and they lasted until the civil rights era. A recent study by the Federal Reserve Bank of Chicago indicates that the schools had a significant impact on raising the educational level of the students who attended them. The schools helped create a new black middle class in the South. Rosenwald had hoped that if blacks and whites within the same community worked together to raise funds for and build a school for blacks, it would break down racial barriers. This did not happen until the civil rights movement advanced in the 1960s, and even then it took many years to erode the prejudices of centuries. But building the schools was an important step on this road to equality.

Peter M. Ascoli, PhD
Chicago, Illinois

"For the well-being of mankind"
—Rosenwald Fund By-Laws

The legacy of the Rosenwald schools continues today. Decades after the last school was built, people remember and honor the positive impact those schools had on their families. Throughout the South, community members are lovingly saving and restoring many of the remaining Rosenwald school buildings. This former Rosenwald school in Sumner County, Tennessee, was dedicated as a community center, with the assistance of the National Trust for Historic Preservation and Lowe's home improvement centers.

Marian Anderson sings
before seventy-five
thousand people at
the Lincoln Memorial
in Washington, D.C.,
April 9, 1939.

10

1 REALIZING THE DREAM

The Rosenwald Fund . . . "came to the aid of Negroes at that time."

—Henry Allen Bullock, historian

On Easter Sunday, April 9, 1939, millions of Americans made themselves comfortable in front of their living room radios. Another seventy-five thousand people, including members of the United States Congress and the Supreme Court, settled into their seats at the Lincoln Memorial in Washington, D.C. They were prepared to enjoy a special concert by Marian Anderson, one of the country's most acclaimed concert singers. The original site for the concert was supposed to be Constitution Hall close by. But at nearly the last moment, the Daughters of the American Revolution (DAR) denied Ms. Anderson the use of their hall. It seems they had overlooked a clause in the contract that prohibited the hall's use by African Americans, like Marian Anderson.

First Lady Eleanor Roosevelt protested the DAR's decision loudly. She not only resigned from the organization but also arranged the move to the Lincoln Memorial. "When I stood up to sing our national anthem," Ms. Anderson later recalled, "I felt for a moment as though I were choking. For a desperate second I thought that the words would not come."

11

Dr. Charles Drew, the "father of the blood bank," conducted groundbreaking research in storing and processing blood. His Rosenwald Fellowship allowed him to advance his education.

Ms. Anderson faced terrible obstacles throughout her life. When she graduated from high school and applied to a music school, she was told, "We don't take coloreds." Discrimination against African Americans was a way of life in the first half of the twentieth century.

But Marian Anderson ended up going to music school in Europe thanks in large part to a financial gift from the Julius Rosenwald Fund.

Charles Drew was an excellent student and athlete at Dunbar High School in Washington, D.C., and earned admission to Amherst College in Massachusetts. He did well there and decided to become a physician after graduation. He was accepted to McGill University in Montreal to study medicine, but a lack of money almost ended his dream. With support from the Rosenwald Fund, he attended McGill and ultimately made lifesaving contributions to the field of medicine with his work on blood transfusions and blood banking.

Other well-known African Americans, including writer James Weldon Johnson and artist Jacob Lawrence, successfully pursued their dreams thanks to the Julius Rosenwald Fund. But it was not only the famous whose lives were dramatically changed by the generosity of the fund.

In the first half of the twentieth century, the Rosenwald Fund was the "most influential philanthropic force that came to aid of Negroes at that time." It provided fellowships to promising young Southern blacks and whites to study at Northern universities. It awarded grants to improve library services and teacher-training institutions for Southern blacks. It supported black universities, including Howard University in Washington, D.C. And it helped build and staff community health clinics and black hospitals.

James Weldon Johnson was a noted author, civil rights leader, and professor. In 1889, he wrote the words to "Lift Ev'ry Voice and Sing," which became the unofficial African American national anthem.

Jacob Lawrence was the best-known African American artist of the twentieth century. His *Migration Series*, depicting the often difficult journey of Southern blacks to Northern cities, was completed between 1940 and 1941 while on a Rosenwald Fellowship. In 1945, while serving in the U.S. Coast Guard during World War II, he attended an exhibition of his work at the Institute of Modern Art in Boston.

But it was the fund's school-building project that had the most profound effect. The lives of hundreds of thousands of young African Americans were forever changed by the 5,357 schools built by the Rosenwald Fund in the Deep South.

Before the first Rosenwald school opened, education for black children in the South was limited by discrimination. At the end of the Civil War, federal troops remained in the South to protect the rights of newly freed slaves. Washington officials urged Southern states to provide public education for all children, black as well as white. Northern churches and other groups initially contributed money to establish schools for children of freed slaves, but it was not enough to make a significant impact.

When federal troops withdrew in 1877, Southern states began passing "Jim Crow" laws, which segregated

continued on page 17

Thomas Nast's *Emancipation*. On either side of this engraving are scenes contrasting black life in the South under slavery with visions of the freeman's life after the Civil War.

King & Baird, Printers, 607 Sansom Street, Philadelphia.

Entered according to Act of Congress, in the year 1865, by J. W. UMPEHENT, in the Clerk's Office of the District Court of the United States, for the Eastern District of Pennsylvania.

Published by S. BOTT. No. 43 South Third Street, Philadelphia, Penna.

Rural schools of all types are poor enough, but the rural negro schools are bad beyond comprehension."

This sketch by Alfred R. Waud appeared in *Harper's Weekly* in 1866, a year after the Civil War ended. Zion School for Colored Children in Charleston, South Carolina, was organized and run by African Americans. More than a thousand pupils attended, which showed

Of the nineteen students enrolled in the "colored" school in Anthoston, Kentucky, in 1916, only seven were in attendance when this photograph was taken. This is not a Rosenwald school but typical of schools for black children in the rural South. The teacher told the photographer that she expected the other students back after the harvest season ended. "Tobacco keeps them out and they are short of hands."

blacks from whites. The phrase originated from a popular song in early nineteenth-century minstrel shows in which white entertainers blackened their faces and performed stereotyped imitations of blacks in song and dance. Blacks were separated from whites in nearly all public places—from trains and buses to schools and water fountains. In 1896, in the case *Plessy v. Ferguson*, the United States Supreme Court ruled in a 7–1 decision that segregation by race did not automatically mean racial discrimination. "Separate but equal"—the separation of the races—became a way of life in the South.

African American schools were separate but far from equal. They suffered from poorly prepared teachers, broken-down buildings, and a profound lack of books and supplies. Some black children attended school for only three months of the year since they had to help their parents work on the land during planting and harvesting seasons. One observer reflected on the black schools he saw in the South: "Rural schools of all types are poor enough, but the rural negro schools are bad beyond comprehension." Another reported, "The negro school-houses are miserable beyond all description. They are usually without comfort, equipment, proper lighting or sanitation."

Fortunately, educational opportunities for Southern African Americans were about to improve thanks to Julius Rosenwald, the wealthy president of Sears, Roebuck and Company, and his friendship with the African American educator Booker T. Washington.

This photo of Augusta and Julius Rosenwald was taken shortly after their marriage in 1890. They raised five children. Gussie was active in a number of charitable organizations and served as national vice president of the Girl Scouts of America. When she died in 1929, the *Chicago Jewish Chronicle* remembered her as a "mother, as a wife and as a public-spirited citizen." A Rosenwald school in Shelby County, Tennessee, was named after her.

2 MAKING MONEY: DOING GOOD

> **"Fortune smiled on me in a big way
> and no one was more surprised than I was myself."**
> —Julius Rosenwald

On October 15, 1874, thousands of people gathered in Springfield, Illinois, to dedicate the Lincoln Monument, the final resting place for President Abraham Lincoln and his family. Civil War veterans in their old uniforms mingled with civilians to pay tribute to Lincoln with military music and long speeches by dignitaries, including President Ulysses S. Grant. Darting in and out of the crowd was a twelve-year-old boy selling *The Illustrated Description of the Lincoln Monument*, the dedication's commemorative pamphlet. He was a real go-getter, and business was brisk. People watching him might easily have concluded he was a natural-born salesperson, and they would not be wrong.

Julius Rosenwald was born in Springfield on August 12, 1862, to Samuel and Augusta Rosenwald, German Jewish immigrants. He grew up in a comfortable middle-class family committed to community service. As a child, Julius worked in his father's clothing store while attending school. He left high school after his second year to become an apprentice to his uncles, clothing manufacturers in New York. As an apprentice, Julius started as a stock clerk and rose to become a traveling salesperson, selling his uncles' brand of men's suits to clothing stores around the country. Five years later, and with their father's support, Rosenwald and his brother went into business for themselves. They opened a small men's clothing store in New York, but the business did not prosper. Rosenwald was not discouraged. He had an idea. He realized that clothing manufacturers located in New York could not easily meet the needs of retail stores in other parts of the country.

In 1885, with support from an uncle and with a cousin as partner, the firm of Rosenwald and Weil opened for business in Chicago. Julius traveled widely throughout the Midwest, selling his firm's suits to men's clothing-store owners. The business grew and Julius prospered. Five years later, he married Augusta (Gussie) Nusbaum, the daughter of another German Jewish family also in the clothing business. Rosenwald told a friend, "The aim of my life is to have an income of $15,000 a year—$5,000 to be used for my personal expenses, $5,000 to be laid aside and $5,000 to go to charity."

In 1894, Rosenwald started a new business with an old friend manufacturing inexpensive men's suits. One of their customers was a growing mail-order company.

Next to the Bible, the Sears, Roebuck catalog was often the only other book in a rural household. People called it the "wish book," as they dreamed of buying the many items offered for sale. Julius Rosenwald felt a great responsibility to his customers. He promised them "satisfaction guaranteed or your money back."

> **"The aim of my life is to have an income of $15,000 a year—$5,000 to be used for my personal expenses, $5,000 to be laid aside and $5,000 to go to charity."**
> **—Julius Rosenwald**

Sears, Roebuck and Company had its beginnings in 1886 when Richard Sears, a railway station agent, began selling watches as a sideline. When the watch business began to thrive, he moved his business from Minneapolis to Chicago and hired watchmaker Alvah C. Roebuck. In 1893, they formed Sears, Roebuck and Company and expanded their watch business to include a variety of products for rural farmers. Unlike other merchants, the company did not have a brick-and-mortar store but relied on widely distributed catalogs to sell its wares. The business grew, but the strain of long workdays and continuing money problems were too much for Roebuck and he withdrew from the company in 1895. Needing a new partner and more money, Sears invited Julius Rosenwald to join the company. After thirteen years, Sears retired and Julius Rosenwald became president.

Rosenwald's position at Sears made him rich, and he decided to use his wealth to help others. He and his wife were influenced by Rabbi Emil Hirsch of Temple Sinai whose teachings of social justice and charity encouraged them to share their wealth with those in need. "Never once in all that time have I left the Temple without feeling that I had carried away some helpful or inspiring lesson which would not have come to me except for having placed myself under such an influence," Rosenwald later recalled. Rosenwald first contributed to local Jewish charities, then to the Michael Reese Hospital and the University of Chicago, where he also became a trustee. He and Gussie also supported Hull House and were close friends of Jane Addams, the settlement house's founder. Hull House provided social and educational training to working-class people, most of whom were recent immigrants. Ms. Addams understood that "civilization is a method of living and an attitude of equal respect for all people." Her philosophy strongly influenced Rosenwald, who began giving to groups whose members also contributed, no matter how little, to support their own organizations.

Rosenwald also supported the YMCA movement. Beginning in England in the 1840s and continuing well into the twentieth century in the United States, thousands of young men left rural lives behind for new opportunities. The Young Men's Christian Association (YMCA) helped these young men, newly arrived to work in the teeming cities, find support and security. The organization focused on sports, physical fitness, employment advice, and child care. The first YMCA in the United States opened in Boston in 1851. Soon there were YMCAs in other major cities, including Chicago. Rosenwald believed in the organization's mission—"to put Christian principles into practice through programs that build healthy spirit, mind and body for all"—and began making small contributions to his local Y. To provide a recreational outlet for his employees, he supported the building of a YMCA near the Sears plant.

In 1910, YMCA leaders began thinking about building a separate facility for African Americans. This was a time of racial segregation in America, and a separate facility was not unusual. They approached Rosenwald, who was impressed with their request, and he surprised them with an incredible offer. He would donate $25,000 to any community in America that could raise $75,000 from white and black donors for the construction of a black YMCA. In the end, twenty-five communities—including Chicago—took him up on his unprecedented offer. These Ys also served as temporary lodgings for blacks, who were not allowed to stay in white hotels.

At a 1911 gathering in Chicago announcing the building of the first African American YMCA, Rosenwald told the audience, "It startled me when I, a Jew, was asked for money to promote the Christian religion but I thought as long as I was going to give money to Africans I would give it here where we have many negro citizens, instead of to foreign missions."

A year earlier, a friend had sent Rosenwald two books that had a profound effect on him. The first book motivated him. *An American Citizen: The Life of William H. Baldwin, Jr.* by John Graham Brooks is the story of a white New England philanthropist who supported educational efforts in the South for African Americans and was a close friend of Booker T. Washington's. After reading the book, Rosenwald wrote: "It is glorious, a story of a man who really *led* a life which is to my liking and whom I shall endeavor to imitate."

The other book inspired him. Dr. Booker T. Washington's *Up from Slavery* is the riveting account of the author's rise from slavery to his leadership of the Tuskegee Institute. Washington was born a slave on a

Booker T. Washington traveled throughout the country speaking about his work and his plans for the future. Here he is shown in Mound Bayou, Mississippi, in 1912.

Virginia plantation in 1856. But even as a young child, he developed a thirst for knowledge. In the book, Booker T. Washington recalled his childhood: "I had no schooling whatever while I was a slave, though I remember on several occasions I went as far as the schoolhouse door with one of my young mistresses to carry her books. The picture of several dozen boys and girls in a schoolroom engaged in study made a deep impression upon me, and I had the feeling that to get into a schoolhouse and study in this way would be about the same as getting into paradise." Washington later wrote: "From the time that I can remember having any thoughts about anything, I recall that I had an intense longing to learn to read."

When the Civil War ended in 1865, young Booker went to work in a salt mine but made time during the workday to go to school. At sixteen years old, he gained admission to Hampton Institute, a Virginia school founded to provide industrial and trade education to recently freed slaves. "At Hampton, for the first time," he wrote in *Up from Slavery*, "I learned what education was expected to do for an individual. Before going there I had a good deal of the then rather prevalent idea among our people that to secure an education meant to have a good, easy time, free from all necessity for manual labour. At Hampton I not only learned that it was not a disgrace to labour, but learned to love labour, not alone for its financial value, but for labour's own sake. . . . I got my first taste of what it meant to live a life of unselfishness, my first knowledge of

This photo shows five generations of a slave family on the Smith plantation in Beaufort, South Carolina, in 1862. Living conditions were poor, and educational opportunities for blacks during slavery were either limited or nonexistent.

the fact that the happiest individuals are those who do the most to make others useful and happy." After graduation, he remained at the school as a teacher.

In 1881, he moved to Alabama to become the first president of the Tuskegee Institute, known then as the Normal School for Colored Teachers. At the institute, he taught that the way for African Americans to become fully integrated into American society was through patience, hard work, and self-reliance. Washington believed that blacks first needed to focus on practical education to establish themselves as good, industrious citizens before the goal of complete equality with whites could be reached. His belief in black self-help appealed to white philanthropists who built the Tuskegee Institute into an important educational center. Washington became a nationally famous and influential African American leader. In 1901, he received an invitation to join President Theodore Roosevelt for dinner at the White House, a singular honor for a black man at that time.

The Tuskegee Institute provided serious, but rare, higher education for African Americans. In this 1902 photograph, science students are conducting laboratory experiments. Much of the science curriculum was focused on improving agricultural techniques.

Rosenwald organized train trips to the Tuskegee Institute to introduce his wealthy friends to the work of Booker T. Washington. On those visits, Rosenwald was treated as an honored guest and friend.

3 WORKING WITH WASHINGTON

> "Julius Rosenwald was the man who gave us public education."
>
> —Mildred Ridgley Gray, student

Dr. Booker T. Washington's philosophy of self-help appealed to Julius Rosenwald. Over time, he believed that charitable organizations should include the participation of recipients. "In the first place philanthropy is a sickening word," Rosenwald once said. "It is generally looked upon as helping a man who hasn't a cent in the world. That sort of thing hardly interests me. I do not like the 'sob stuff' philanthropy. What I want to do is to try and cure the things that seem to be wrong." He thought that people could not fully appreciate gifts automatically handed them; if they participated, even a little, in helping themselves, they would feel the pride of ownership.

Rosenwald agreed with Washington that there was only one way to improve the lives of African Americans. Blacks needed access to schooling in trades and skills. That would lead to meaningful jobs, allowing them to advance economically and socially. Washington knew that many people living in the

Julius Rosenwald contributed $250,000 to the University of Chicago for the construction of a building with the stipulation that the school first raise two-thirds of the necessary funds. Rosenwald Hall was built in 1914. The philanthropist, ever humble, was actually angry with the university for naming the building after him.

In 1926, Julius Rosenwald contributed $3 million to establish the Museum of Science and Industry in Chicago. When it opened in 1933, people first called it the Rosenwald Industrial Museum, although Rosenwald insisted that his name not appear on the building. Today, it remains one of the finest interactive museums in the world.

South worked on farms, so education for blacks had to focus on agricultural skills.

When Booker T. Washington visited Chicago on May 18, 1911, to deliver a speech marking the fifty-third anniversary of Chicago's white YMCA, Julius Rosenwald hosted a luncheon in his honor at Chicago's famous Blackstone Hotel. It was the first time the hotel entertained an African American. In his introduction of the Tuskegee educator, Rosenwald said, "He is helping his own race to attain the high art of self-help and self-dependence, and he is helping the white race to learn that opportunity and obligation go hand in hand."

Rosenwald, reflecting on his Jewish background, then offered a personal insight to his own thinking. "I belong to a people who have known centuries of persecution," he told the assembly, "or whether it is because I am naturally inclined to sympathize with the oppressed, I have always felt keenly for the colored race. . . . The two races must occupy one country." Before leaving Chicago, Washington invited Rosenwald to visit the Tuskegee Institute.

Five months later, Julius Rosenwald, accompanied by his wife, Rabbi Hirsch, and a number of friends, arrived at Tuskegee in a rented train car. The entire school community welcomed them warmly, and for four days the visitors toured the facilities and spoke to students. Rosenwald was impressed with what he saw and accepted Washington's invitation to join the institute's board of directors. "I don't believe," Rosenwald said, "there is a white industrial school in America or anywhere that compares to Mr. Washington's at Tuskegee."

Washington was not shy about making known the financial needs of the school, but Rosenwald was cautious. When he returned to Chicago, Rosenwald sent his first donation, a shipment of shoes and hats from Sears, Roebuck for the students. Although it was not the gift he expected, Washington responded with a letter of thanks. Over time, there were other such shipments. Gradually, his relationship with Washington grew stronger and Rosenwald began making cash contributions to the school. Rosenwald also arranged train trips to Tuskegee from Chicago to encourage other wealthy and influential citizens to support the school. In turn, Booker T. Washington returned to Chicago on fund-raising trips and stayed at the Rosenwald home.

On August 12, 1912, in honor of his fiftieth birthday, Rosenwald gave a number of gifts to institutions he favored. Jewish Charities of Chicago and the University of Chicago each received $250,000 in matching grants. Other grants established a home for Jewish orphans and a tuberculosis sanitarium. A smaller grant of $25,000 went to Dr. Washington, who asked to use a portion of the money to build several elementary schools near

Tuskegee. Washington was deeply concerned about the terrible state of education for young black children in the South. The schools, he observed, "are as bad as stables."

Rosenwald, who once said, "It is almost always easier to make a million dollars honestly than to dispose of it

The title for this cartoon of Rosenwald's fiftieth birthday party read "Other Millionaires Please Note—this Form of Birthday Party is not Copyrighted." The announcement of the gifts Rosenwald gave for his birthday drew public applause. Note the words in the cartoon, "Give While You Live," which represented Rosenwald's philosophy.

> **"It is almost always easier to make a million dollars honestly than to dispose of it wisely."**
> **—Julius Rosenwald**

wisely," looked into Washington's request and discovered that the majority of blacks who lived in the South had little chance of receiving any meaningful education. He found that in white schools there was one teacher for thirty students, while in the black community one teacher was responsible for more than two hundred students. Macon County, home of Tuskegee Institute, spent $14 for the education of each white child and only 20¢ for each black child. Rosenwald was shocked and quickly agreed to Booker T. Washington's request. The only requirement was that each community had to contribute to the building of the school. Rosenwald strongly believed that, by participating in raising money, everyone would feel a sense of pride and ownership.

The first Rosenwald school was built in Loachapoka, Alabama, in 1913, not far from Tuskegee.

The total cost of the school was $942.50; Rosenwald's contribution was $300. The remaining funds came from local blacks in cash and labor and from local white citizens. A major requirement was that state and county authorities had to maintain the school as a regular part of the public school system. Within months, five more schools were built. Booker T. Washington wrote to Rosenwald after the school dedications: "The people showed in a very acceptable way their gratitude to you for what you are helping them to do." Pleased with this initial success, the Sears, Roebuck president gave money to help build 80 more schools. This was just the beginning of what would become Julius Rosenwald's most important legacy. Over the next two decades, he would be responsible for helping to build more than 5,300 schools.

Industrial and agricultural education were not unique to the first Rosenwald schools. In this 1902 photograph taken ten years before the first Rosenwald school was built, students at the Annie Davis School near Tuskegee, Alabama, learn about corn and cotton.

Eli Madison
Founder

Farmers Club
Madison Park

Madison
Park

The Old and New

The Madison Park School in Montgomery County, Alabama, was one of the first six Rosenwald schools built under the direction of the Tuskegee Institute in 1913–1914. The community was founded around 1880 by a group of fourteen former slaves led by Eli and Frank Madison. Booker T. Washington sent Rosenwald photos of these earliest schools, which Rosenwald found

4 TURNING DREAMS INTO REALITY

"Those who are happiest are those who do the most for others."
—Booker T. Washington

The first schools were designed

and built under the supervision of the Tuskegee Institute staff members, who developed plans that fit the needs of individual communities. Three building types were created: one- and two-teacher schools, a consolidated school that merged several local schools into one, and a county training school that served students from a wide geographic area. Each school plan reflected the Tuskegee philosophy and included an area for industrial education. The buildings were not known by the number of rooms but by the number of teachers. The Tuskegee staff constructed the earliest schools as one- or two-teacher buildings. Even a one-teacher school contained an academic classroom, an industrial classroom, a kitchen, and coatrooms. There were no bathrooms inside the buildings. Instead, sanitary privies (toilets) were placed outside.

The train trips gave Rosenwald an opportunity to meet Tuskegee students and see the new elementary schools in action. On this trip, in 1915, he visited Rosenwald schools for the first time. Crowds greet the Rosenwalds enthusiastically at the train station.

During the 1915 trip to the Tuskegee Institute, Julius Rosenwald is shown at the dedication of the Big Zion School, one of the first six Rosenwald schools built in Alabama under the direction of the institute staff.

In February 1915, Julius Rosenwald took another train trip to Tuskegee with a group of donors to see the new schools. Their train arrived in Montgomery, Alabama, and the travelers set out on the sixty-mile trip to Tuskegee in a fleet of automobiles. As they stopped to view each newly built school, they were greeted by enthusiastic groups of children and adults, white and black. Rosenwald noticed that homes near the schools were freshly painted or whitewashed, a clear sign that the new schools increased community pride. Rosenwald spoke at each school and

The first schools were built with Rosenwald money under the supervision of the Tuskegee Institute. Later, the designs were improved by the Rosenwald Fund. Visits by Rosenwald were a time for community celebrations. In this photo, people in Montgomery County, Alabama, await the arrival of Julius Rosenwald for the dedication of the Davenport School in 1915.

Davenport

"expressed his appreciation of the wonderful things that the pupils and teachers had done for themselves."

But these building accomplishments were soon overshadowed by the sudden death of Booker T. Washington from high blood pressure on November 14, 1915. He was just fifty-nine years of age. Despite this tragic loss, Rosenwald and the Tuskegee Institute staff decided to continue the school-building project.

Two years later, the fast-growing number of schools and the amount of work needed to build, staff, and supervise them overwhelmed the few Tuskegee employees. A lack of supervision led some contractors to cut corners by using inferior materials or accepting shoddy workmanship. Sometimes, local workers had difficulty reading blueprints or safely fitting stoves. Concerned with the situation, Rosenwald assumed direct responsibility from the Tuskegee staff to oversee all school construction projects. And to manage all the school-related responsibilities, he created the Julius Rosenwald Fund "for the well-being of mankind."

Using the original Tuskegee plans as models, the fund began to set stricter standards in all aspects of school building.

Rosenwald urged—not always successfully—white public officials to spend equal, even if still separate, amounts for the education of black and white children. The goal was to increase public responsibility for maintaining local schools and decrease contributions from the Rosenwald Fund. Some white citizens realized the benefit of a Rosenwald school in their community and contributed money. Quite often, white landowners donated the land for a school. Black citizens donated their labor or whatever money they could.

Schools were also required to stay open at least five months a year. Booker T. Washington once said, "Negro children may be smart but the white people of the South compliment them too much when they think they can learn in four months as much as white children can in nine."

As the school-building project grew, the fund developed new designs and stricter requirements for

In 1922, Julius Rosenwald won a Chicago newspaper's motto contest. The cash award to the now multimillionaire was five dollars. More importantly, the quote he submitted, by Robert Ingersoll, summed up Rosenwald's life: "I would rather be a beggar and spend my money like a king than a king and spend my money like a beggar."

the school buildings. These were published in 1924, and copies of *Community School Plans* were distributed to interested groups. The book provided specific details, some described on pages 40–43, on all aspects of a building project.

continued on page 40

The old "colored" school in Burgin, Kentucky, shown in 1919 just before it was replaced by a new Rosenwald building

Workers install window frames for a new Rosenwald school in Gregg County, Texas, March 1921 (above and top right). Because the early schools did not have electricity, the Rosenwald Fund's *Community School Plans* required that all schools be built facing east or west to get the most natural light. Throughout the South, a Rosenwald school could always be identified by its large banks of windows.

This worn-down shack served as a school for black children in Bienville Parish, Louisiana. It was replaced by a

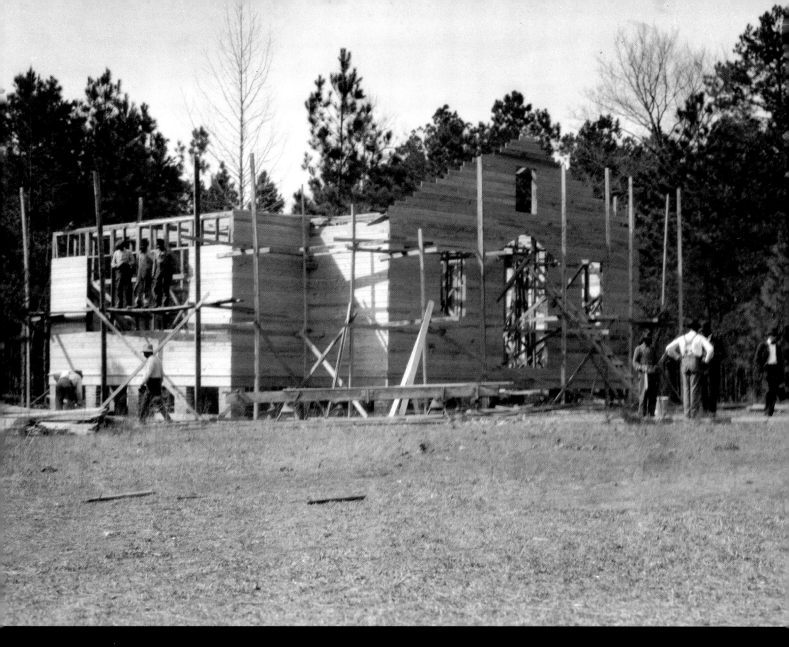

Construction on the new Rosenwald school in Bienville Parish, Louisiana, was done by local residents who contributed their

Choosing a site: Each school was located near a highway and a population center, and the land measured at least two acres in size for a one- or two-teacher school. The site included enough space for agricultural projects and landscaping. Since most schools had no access to electricity, classroom windows faced east or west to increase the amount of natural light in the classroom. The designers chose tan window shades instead of the traditional green shades to allow more light to enter the room. And to provide even more light, the plans book also required that "care should be taken to see that at least one foot at the top of the window is never covered."

Planning and constructing the building:
Communities received detailed blueprints for their schools, but building materials were not supplied. This was a conscious decision of the Rosenwald Fund. Rosenwald did not want people to think that Sears profited from his school program. (Sears, Roebuck and Company was known for selling complete home-building kits.) He also thought it better for community relations to allow local merchants to provide the building materials.

The Rosenwald Fund set the strict requirements, but the day-to-day construction and supervision of the schools were the responsibilities of state building agents—all white men at first—

who were employees of each state's board of education. To build one hundred Rosenwald schools in Alabama, Julius Rosenwald gave $1,500 to the state to hire a "well-trained Negro" to assist the state agent. Soon there were African American Rosenwald Building Agents who worked directly with the local communities, the only blacks in the South officially part of their state education departments.

The school was made large enough to accommodate future growth. Specific contracts were drawn with builders and suppliers to guarantee that the building met all the specific requirements as set down in the Rosenwald plans. Communities chose between two interior color schemes: buff walls and walnut wainscoting or light gray walls and walnut-stain wainscoting. Either one provided sufficient light. Painters used non-gloss paint so "as not to injure the eyes of the teacher and pupils who must remain inside the classrooms for six hours or more each day."

In keeping with Booker T. Washington's wishes, an industrial room was planned for each building so the schools would "provide [not] only formal and theoretical 'book larnin' but also practical work. . . . Girls were expected to learn sewing and cooking and the boys farming and simple work with tools." Since modern bathrooms did not exist in

The first Rosenwald Building Agents, 1916. Seated is C. J. Calloway, the first general field agent.

Building a Rosenwald school in Milliken's Bend, Louisiana. The one- and two-teacher schools were the easiest and fastest to build. There was no electricity, running water, or plumbing to worry about.

many rural areas, "improved sanitation for better health was a major concern of all of the Rosenwald school planners in the 1910s and early 1920s." Plans provided for the construction of privies—outdoor toilets. Later, the plans included indoor bathrooms.

Landscaping: The plans provided instructions on how to build walkways, prepare the ground for landscaping, and even create the right mixture of grass seed for planting. "Make walks wide enough so that two persons can comfortably walk side by side on them. . . . Any steep slope or terrace should be sodded with blue grass sod or Bermuda grass sod, carefully placed, tamped, and pegged."

Equipping the school: White community leaders often tried to save money by equipping Rosenwald schools with used blackboards and student desks from white schools. The Rosenwald Fund clearly insisted on brand-new furnishings. The local community was also responsible for the building's upkeep and for school supplies.

With detailed plans now in place, it was time to expand the Rosenwald school program. Throughout the South, black parents worked hard to bring Rosenwald schools to their communities. They knew that education would mean more opportunities and, they hoped, brighter futures for their children.

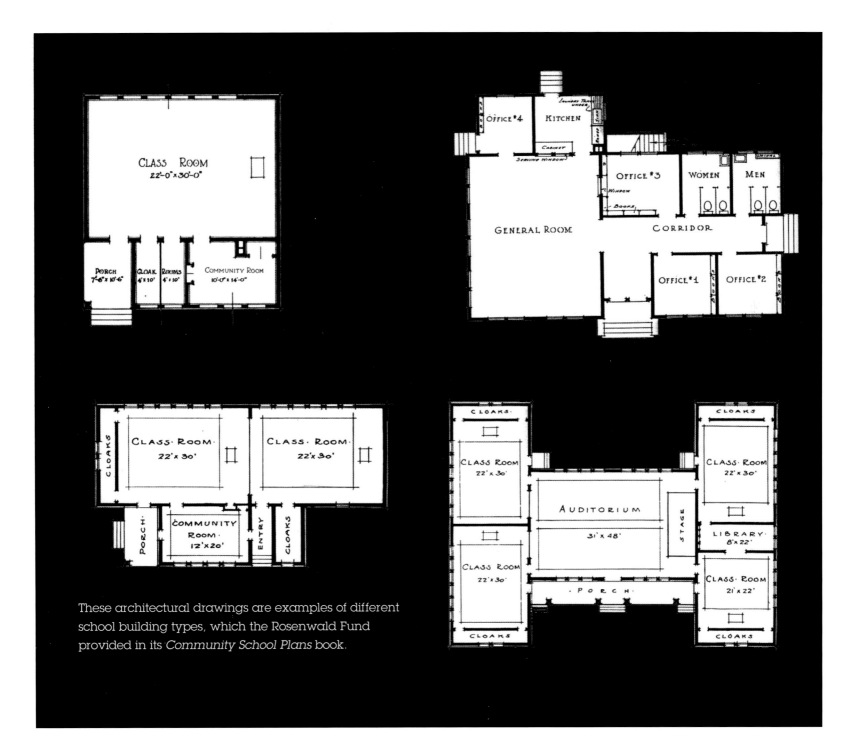

These architectural drawings are examples of different school building types, which the Rosenwald Fund provided in its *Community School Plans* book.

Teacher and students inside the two-teacher Coletown Elementary School, built in 1920–1921, in Fayette County, Kentucky.

5 THE ROSENWALD PATCH

"Considering all the things we didn't have while attending Rosenwald, I remember all the things we had, and we were happy still."

—Audrey Hutchison, student

Fund-raising became a community-

wide lesson in cooperation. Before receiving Rosenwald Fund grants, each local community had to raise an equal sum of money. It would not be easy. Rural blacks in the South were poor, and with little cash, they had to find other ways to realize their dreams of a better future for their children.

A flyer announcing a "Financial Educational Rally" in 1929 invited African Americans in one community to join with their neighbors to hear from "prominent visitors." Some were enticed by the words "free dinner served." But the flyer impressed the seriousness of the event upon everyone. "Realizing the fact that the only medium through which any race can achieve success is by its people, we are inviting every community, school and church to be present in order that our goal might be successfully reached."

From the beginning, the Rosenwald schools emphasized industrial education. The skills learned in shop classes often resulted in handcrafted items that students could sell. In this photograph, students proudly display samples of their work in front of the Newton School in Calcasieu Parish, Louisiana.

Many blacks in the South grew up without an education and did not trust the promises of white people. But once African Americans realized that a new school could become a reality, they set to work raising funds. In community after community, "they saved by eating even less than their usual meager diet. They sold their tiny surplus wherever they could—a few eggs here, a hen there, a bit of their corn crop. And they put away every penny." Children did odd jobs and saved the earned pennies. Some families sold off parts of their farms. In one town, a former slave contributed his life savings—$36 in pennies—"so that his great-grandchildren might have a chance to be educated." Those who had nothing to contribute volunteered their time and labor to actually build the school.

One woman recalled, "We gave parties . . . big picnics, dinners and they [the people who came] would donate that money to us for Rosenwald School, and we raised enough money. We raised $800. . . . Of course, our preacher and them kind of criticized us for having dances and things, but after all, it was doing good for the community. . . . And we had a four-room school."

In Autauga County, Alabama, "children without shoes on their feet gave from fifty cents to one dollar and old men and old women, whose costumes represented several years of wear, gave from one to five dollars." When they realized they still were more than a thousand dollars off the goal, "colored men offered to pawn their cows. . . . They made notes and gave for security pledges on their future crops . . . and other belongings for the money."

In another Alabama county, schoolchildren were given small boxes to fill with coins. When the children raised more than $200 (some by chopping cotton in the heat of the day), their parents and other community adults—"men who worked at furnaces, women who washed and ironed for white people"—held a rally and raised the necessary additional funds. Often, the money-raising activities centered within a local black church that supported the building of the school and later provided needed supplies and equipment. People "sponsored socials and taffy pulls, events in which Negro patrons at every level of income could pay a small amount of money and participate."

In even poorer communities, where residents had little or no cash, "men went to the woods, cut down trees, hauled them to the saw mill and had them cut into lumber. Others cleared away the grounds, and even women worked carrying water, and feeding the men while they labored until enough material was placed on the grounds for the two-teacher building." Other residents, even those without children, mortgaged their own homes and farms to contribute the money necessary to complete school buildings.

In other places, farmers set aside parts of their fields, which became known as "Rosenwald Patches," and contributed to their school-building fund from the crops grown on these patches.

Each new building presented challenges, some more serious than others. In Warren County, Mississippi, the local Ku Klux Klan threatened to prevent the construction of schools. The Klan, a secret group of white Americans, fought to keep blacks and other minorities from attaining equal rights. The Klan's hatred of blacks extended to the school superintendent, who was Catholic, and the school board, because two of its members were Jewish. The superintendent, John H. Culkin, organized plans to keep the Klan off guard. He ordered the lumber and construction materials for the twenty-five planned county schools and arranged for them to be delivered by rail on a specific date known only by a few. Supportive white citizens not only contributed money to the project but, when the railroad cars arrived, also supplied 160 mule teams and wagons to pick up and deliver the building materials to the planned sites throughout the county. At each site, local children were organized in advance to clear out rocks and remove rubbish. Women cooked and served meals to the workers,

A former slave contributed his life savings . . . "so that his great-grandchildren might have a chance to be educated."

The four-teacher Barbee School in Bolivar County, Mississippi, built in 1927–1928. It was funded by $2,600 contributed by blacks, $900 by whites, $1,000 by public taxes, and $1,000 by the Rosenwald Fund.

who began construction as soon as the materials arrived. "Within a month all had been completed, painted inside and out, equipped, and ready for use."

Once a school was built, attention turned to maintaining the building. By the late 1920s, each of the Southern states with Rosenwald schools held annual Rosenwald School Days. Each day served as a way not only to raise money for the school's upkeep but also to show the progress of the students and give thanks for the special educational opportunity offered to the community. The State Board of Education in Virginia decreed that during the month of March 1929, a day

The three-teacher Bogue Chitto School in Lincoln County, Mississippi, built in 1923–1924, included a library and a teacher home. It was built with $5,200 from blacks, $1,100 from whites, $2,000 from public taxes, and $1,500 from the Rosenwald Fund.

"be set aside in each county known as Rosenwald Day on which day all schools in the County shall observe by an appropriate celebration." In Brunswick County, that day was March 22. The president of the Brunswick School League and Teachers' Association asked "that people in each school community attend the meeting to show their appreciation of Mr. Rosenwald's interest in us, which has enabled our county to build more Rosenwald Schools than any county in the State (15) in number."

White communities usually did not object to the Rosenwald schools. Some mistakenly believed that the Rosenwald Fund totally paid for the school buildings

Before the United States entered World War I in 1917, President Woodrow Wilson named Rosenwald to the Advisory Commission of the Council of National Defense. In 1918, Rosenwald went to Europe to visit army supply units. One particular day, he joined high-ranking officers to greet his friend, Newton Baker, the secretary of war. As each of the decorated generals and colonels was introduced, Rosenwald, the Sears, Roebuck president, dressed in a plain uniform without insignia, stepped forward and introduced himself as General Merchandise.

and upkeep and that no local money was involved. Some simply believed that providing good education for African Americans was the right thing to do. In Mount Dora, Florida, the Reverend Duncan C. Milner, a white minister, contributed enough money to build a school. To honor him, the school was named the Milner-Rosenwald Academy.

Others thought that a Rosenwald school was nothing more than good business. Because black workers were a source of cheap farm labor, white landowners thought that the new schools might keep black families in their communities. This was a time when increasing numbers of black families were leaving the South in a Great Migration to Northern cities for work opportunities and better living conditions. (The number of European immigrants decreased during World War II. So Northern manufacturers looked to the South—where nearly 90 percent of black Americans lived—for needed workers.) For the remaining families, the Rosenwald schools provided students with agricultural and mechanical skills that translated into decent jobs in the South.

Each Rosenwald school had an industrial room where students learned those valuable skills and followed the beliefs of Booker T. Washington, who said, "Textbooks should be subordinated to activities and the recitation room will be the farm, the shop, the home. Classroom work will be based largely upon what the students are doing in the trades and home economics classes."

From the beginning, Julius Rosenwald himself oversaw the work of the fund that bore his name. But in 1928, after eleven years of directing the school program, he realized that he needed more time for his other philanthropic interests and changed the way the fund operated. He believed that his fund needed new leadership with an independent board of trustees. He gave up his position as president but remained as chairman of the board. The new president was Edwin R. Embree, who Rosenwald personally recruited from the Rockefeller Foundation, another important charitable organization. To mark the change, Rosenwald donated twenty thousand shares of Sears, Roebuck and Company stock to the fund, but he made one surprising request of the new board of trustees: all money controlled by the fund had to be spent within twenty-five years of his death. He could make this decision because all the fund's money came from his own wealth.

Julius and Gussie Rosenwald aboard the SS *Aquitania* in 1926 during one of a number of trips to Europe. Gussie was fully supportive of her husband's philanthropy and often traveled with him. She died in 1929. A year later, Julius married Adelaide Rau Goodkind.

Teachers at a Rosenwald school in Ashley County, Arkansas, 1924. In Southern rural communities, the teachers in Rosenwald schools served as positive role models for students. Some of these men and women were poorly educated, but they did their best to ensure brighter futures for the children they taught.

6 EVERYONE WAS SO PROUD

"When this building was finished, it was a state of the art. We were very proud of it."

—Dr. Penny Perry, student

The Rosenwald School built in Drew County, Arkansas, in 1924 was a typical building. The two classrooms were divided by a movable wall that could be opened for community events. The industrial room was outfitted with a sewing machine, washtubs, and ironing boards and irons to teach girls homemaking skills. With no inside plumbing, the children used two outhouses. One student recalled that without toilet paper, they relied on cutout pages from old Sears, Roebuck catalogs. The schools had a positive effect not only on the students but also on their parents and their communities. A student later said, "At least if you got educated, you could fight for yourself and start applying for jobs that were reserved for whites."

In many schools, a portrait of Julius Rosenwald was prominently displayed, even though Rosenwald did not want his name attached to the

Along with the usual classes in reading and writing, some schools provided extra activities such as sports and drama for their students. After performing a play with a Spanish theme, these students pose in front of the Rosenwald School in Manchester, Tennessee, in 1929. The community was proud of the school's drama program and raised money to purchase the school's stage curtain.

buildings. Despite his wish, all the schools he funded, even those named after others, were simply called Rosenwald schools.

The new Rosenwald schools were clean, inviting, and bright—vast improvements over the schools they replaced. Students were happy to be there and eager to learn. For many, it was the first time they could sit at desks rather than rough plank benches.

But not everything improved. When the schools were being built, the Rosenwald Fund insisted that all

> # "In the mornings it was cold," one student later recalled, "and it was very difficult to concentrate."

the furniture and equipment had to be new. But after the schools opened, local school boards maintained the building and provided books and supplies. To save money, some school boards passed down older textbooks from white schools. One former Rosenwald student recalled, "You could never finish a story, the back pages were always torn out." Even so, there often weren't enough books to pass around, so students shared with classmates who sat nearby.

Some schools were also poorly heated. The large windows provided plenty of sunshine, but the usual coal- or wood-burning stoves had to be constantly fed and did not provide much heat. Students near the stove were too warm, and those farther away were cold most of the day. "In the mornings it was cold," one student later recalled, "and it was very difficult to concentrate."

The school day often began with the Pledge of Allegiance or with a religious hymn. The school curriculum contained lessons in reading, writing, spelling, and arithmetic along with time for industrial education. Recess was held outside in good weather.

Qualified African American teachers were hard to find in the early years, and teachers often came from outside the rural communities where the schools were built. At first, they would be on a housing rotation, spending a few weeks at a time as guests in student homes. Later, the Rosenwald Fund sponsored separate teacher homes in communities with larger schools. These teacher houses were convenient and allowed teachers to remain at school longer to help their students.

Although most students were well behaved, there were always a few who were not. One student recalled her teacher at the Cairo Rosenwald School in Gallatin, Tennessee: "She had boys in there bigger than she was, but she didn't have any problems. She had a little hickory stick. Back then, you could whip the kids." Another student remembered, "If the teachers told your parents you had acted up, you got it when you got home."

But Rosenwald teachers were dedicated to their schools and students, despite salaries that were lower than those of white teachers. Because they had no additional staff, both teachers and students pitched in to take care of the school. The work wasn't easy. A boy remembered, "The teacher would send us out in the woods with a burlap bag to find some wood. We'd come back and our hands would be so cold and we would stick them in water." At the Hope Rosenwald School in Pomaria, South Carolina, boys walked a mile to a small store to bring back buckets of water for drinking and hand-washing.

Students and teachers found imaginative ways to pay for supplies. One former student of the Columbia (Texas) Rosenwald School recalled, "There were a lot of pecan trees around the school. The teacher would have us pick up pecans and she sold them and bought us a baseball and bats and gloves. Then we could play baseball." At the Brevard (North Carolina) Rosenwald School, students saved ice-cream wrappers, which were redeemed for balls or board games.

As the school-building project continued to grow, no one could imagine it ending. The Rosenwald Fund depended on Sears, Roebuck stock for its income. But when the stock market crashed in 1929, leading to the Great Depression, the company's stock price plunged in value. The economy was shattered, businesses and jobs disappeared, and fund trustees changed direction. In 1930, the Rosenwald Fund ended aid for building the rural one-teacher schools and a year later for two-teacher schools. After building 5,357 schools, the Rosenwald School Building Program ended officially in 1932. By then, more than "one-fourth of all the black schoolchildren in the

Years before he was president, Franklin Delano Roosevelt (FDR) discussed with the fund staff about building a school in Warm Springs, Georgia, his second home. Afflicted with polio, he had been visiting Warm Springs since 1924 to be treated in the town's famous warm waters. FDR was embarrassed by the condition of the school for black children there. On March 18, 1937, five years after the fund's building program officially ended, FDR proudly delivered the keynote address at the dedication ceremony of the new Eleanor Roosevelt School, named after his wife.

South were taught in Rosenwald schools." But even though no more rural schools were built, the existing schools continued to provide education for decades to come.

The fund began building larger regional, consolidated schools that offered more courses, employed more teachers, and served more students. Since many students had to travel long distances, "the Fund provided 270 buses, which transported ten thousand Black students eight thousand miles daily in 128 counties of

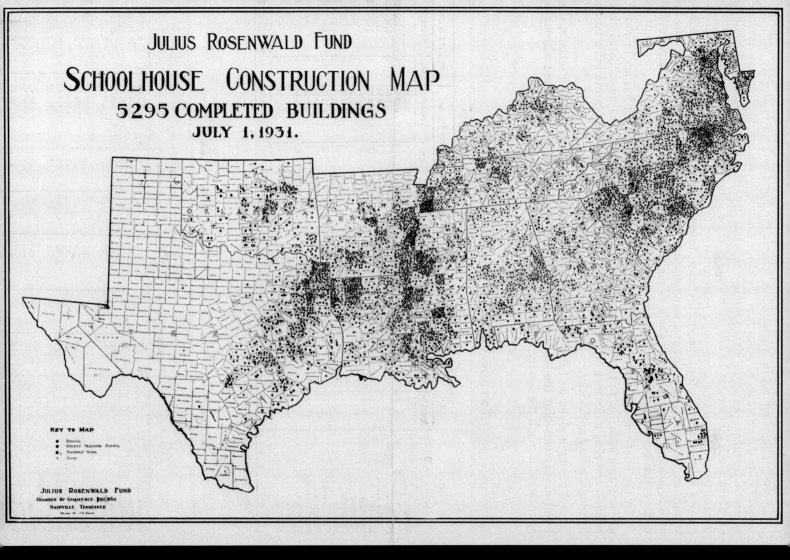

JULIUS ROSENWALD FUND

SCHOOLHOUSE CONSTRUCTION MAP

5295 COMPLETED BUILDINGS
JULY 1, 1931.

KEY TO MAP
- SCHOOL
- COUNTY TRAINING SCHOOL
- TEACHERS' HOME
- SHOP

JULIUS ROSENWALD FUND
CHAMBER OF COMMERCE BUILDING
NASHVILLE, TENNESSEE.

Each year, the Rosenwald Fund updated a map indicating where the Rosenwald schools were located. This is the last map issued in 1932 as the Rosenwald Fund ended its rural school building program.

thirteen Southern states." But there was an important catch. Local school authorities had to lengthen the school term to eight months and, after a three-year period, assume all the costs for student transportation.

The fund also built five large industrial high schools in Southern states. These schools provided older black students with not only solid general education but also shop skills they could use when they graduated. Years later, a former Rosenwald student fondly recalled her school experience: "The Rosenwald training was like going to heaven," she said. "It put a star in my life."

By 1931, Edwin R. Embree, the fund's president, began to reconsider his thinking about the way students best learn. "The purpose of formal education," he said, was not to "cram knowledge into the child but . . . to find ways to stimulate his interest, to help him get started in the most effective way on the road of learning." That year, he wrote to Julius Rosenwald, "My own guess is that the thing to do is give students good fundamental general education and then let them learn the tricks of their trades on the job."

In 1934, the fund further expanded its mission and created the Council on Rural Education to examine and improve the quality of education in all rural schools, black and white. The fund no longer focused on the quantity of schools but became concerned with the quality of learning in the classrooms. To observe what was really happening in the schools, the council hired sixteen young people, black and white "explorers," to spend extended time in rural communities. What the explorers discovered confirmed Embree's beliefs. They found many schools with bored students and outdated textbooks. They also observed poorly prepared teachers who emphasized rote learning—penmanship, basic arithmetic drills, and reading without comprehension. As well, they discovered that many black schools no longer taught the industrial skills that Booker T. Washington and Julius Rosenwald originally advocated. Many industrial rooms had been turned into cloakrooms or storage facilities.

The fund created teacher-training programs at traditionally black colleges and established "Negro University Centers" at colleges in Washington, D.C., Nashville, Atlanta, and New Orleans. And to make sure that rural classrooms had qualified teachers, the fund leaders identified and supported college students willing to build careers in rural education. For teachers unable to travel to one of these centers, the fund paid for materials and local conferences to improve teacher education.

While students needed qualified teachers, they also needed good books. The fund recognized that rural elementary schools, black and white, lacked not only library books but, in most cases, even basic textbooks. Working with professional librarians, the fund created book collections and offered to pay one-third of the cost as long as the community and the state department of education also each contributed one-third. From 1928 to 1948, "over 12,000 library sets were

The Julius Rosenwald Fund placed great importance on the training of professional teachers. Here, students at the Practice School at Florida Agricultural and Mechanical College in Tallahassee are observing a sample lesson.

distributed, more than half a million books, to schools in all the southern states." For the first few years, because of a lack of black professional librarians, the fund even paid white state librarians to visit black schools and teach students and teachers how to best use and care for the books. In the entire South, there was only one library school for blacks, and that opened in 1925. The Hampton Institute Library School in Hampton, Virginia, was supported by the Carnegie Corporation, the American Library Association, and the Julius Rosenwald Fund. Its graduates then went on to serve in black school and college libraries throughout the South.

The Rosenwald Fund also offered to pay one-third of the cost of new books for the libraries of black colleges, which had to pay the rest. Each college also had to outfit the library with appropriate bookshelves and library furniture and employ a fully trained librarian.

Since few rural residents, white or black, had access to a local public library, the Rosenwald Fund tried a five-year experiment. The fund provided money to libraries in a number of Southern counties with a few specific requirements. First, each county had to hire only trained librarians and provide them with housing. Second, Rosenwald Fund money could be used only to purchase books. Third, in keeping with Julius Rosenwald's beliefs, counties had to provide equal service to both whites and blacks. The experiment was successful, and when it ended in 1935, most counties continued to provide these library services on their own. The counties were also encouraged to place branch libraries in schools to give students easier access to books.

The fund also realized that promising young writers, artists, and scientists needed help to succeed. Until the fund went out of business in 1948, more than 1,500 Rosenwald Fellowships were awarded to promising young writers, artists, scientists, and intellectuals. A thousand of them were African American. The fund believed that by supporting promising black individuals to develop their talents, they would contribute to society and break down the barriers of discrimination. Civil rights leader Julian Bond called those who received the fellowships a "Who's Who of black America in the 1930s and 1940s."

The fund also understood good health was just as important as a good education. At the time, African Americans in the South had limited access to medical care. Few hospitals would even admit them. To improve health conditions, the fund helped build black hospitals and clinics and provided grants to train and hire African American doctors and nurses. By 1942, more than three hundred black public health nurses were practicing in the South. Years before, there were fewer than thirty.

Since its beginnings, the Rosenwald Fund created many different ways to improve the lives of African Americans in the South. It was an ongoing mission. In a 1941 speech at Yale University, Edwin Embree explained why. "No race or class can be firmly assured of fair play so long as we continue to treat any group unfairly."

Dr. Kenneth B. Clark (second from left) stands with NAACP Legal Defense Fund lawyers outside the U.S. District Court House (Eastern District) in Richmond, Virginia, during the *Davis v. County School Board of Prince Edward County* desegregation case in 1952. Dr. Clark and his wife, Dr. Mamie Clark, both psychologists, each had received a Rosenwald Fellowship early in their careers. As part of their work with children, the Clarks used black and white dolls in their research. Their tests proved that self-esteem of black children suffered in a segregated society by generating a "feeling of inferiority as to their status in the community." The children thought the white dolls were "nice" and the black dolls "bad." The work of Kenneth and Mamie Clark provided the U.S. Supreme Court with the "modern authority" to overturn *Plessy v. Ferguson.*

Several "pioneers of American industry" were honored at a banquet in 1928 held in the Hotel Astor in New York City. Among them were, left to right: Harvey Firestone, the founder of Firestone Tire and Rubber Company; Julius Rosenwald; Thomas Edison, whose inventions modernized the world; and Sir Thomas Lipton, the tea merchant and sportsman.

7 CURING THINGS: ROSENWALD'S LEGACY

"What I want to do is to try and cure the things that seem to be wrong."
—Julius Rosenwald

Julius Rosenwald died on January 6, 1932. At his bedside were Adelaide, his second wife, and his five children. The marker at the foot of his grave simply reads "Julius, August 12, 1862–January 6, 1932." From the White House, President Herbert Hoover offered a heartfelt tribute. "One of his most conspicuous contributions to the public welfare was through his humanitarian activities. . . . The foundation which he created for the 'well-being of mankind' constitutes a monument to his vision, sympathy and generosity."

At a memorial service at Nashville's Fisk University, writer James Weldon Johnson, who received a Rosenwald Fellowship, said, "Julius Rosenwald used his brains in disposing of money. Had he used them only in acquiring it, we should not be gathered here."

Some people then and now consider Rosenwald's—and Booker T. Washington's—educational views as somehow racist because they supported the notion of "separate but equal" instead of challenging it. By the early 1900s, younger black leaders, including W. E. B. Du Bois, began attacking Washington's philosophy. They urged blacks to move away from vocational training to pursue more intellectual learning and become active in the political process to attain equal rights. Yet even Du Bois noted that "the death of Julius Rosenwald brings to an end a career remarkable especially for its significance to American Negroes. As a Jew, Julius Rosenwald did not have to be initiated into the methods of race prejudice."

An unusual philanthropist, Julius Rosenwald did not fully fund projects but expected the recipients of his gifts to contribute. He also did not want his money carried over to future generations. Rosenwald believed that wealthy people in each generation should support "such educational, benevolent, or humanitarian enterprises as will benefit their contemporaries." When the work of the Julius Rosenwald Fund ended in 1948, Edwin R. Embree, the fund's longtime president wrote: "All the Fund's work was in faith: faith that if people were given a chance they would grow to their highest stature; faith that in spite of abuses Americans wanted democracy; faith that generations to come would take up the torch and travel the road to a creative society in

Rosenwald (above) was a friend and supporter of President Herbert Hoover. Both strongly believed that businesspeople should honor their social responsibilities and work to help those in need. They first met during World War I when they served together on committees in Washington. Rosenwald campaigned for Hoover during the 1928 presidential election and, after Hoover's election, was an overnight guest at the White House.

which people may achieve their full dignity as human beings and all may find that life is good."

Thanks to the contributions of the Julius Rosenwald Fund:

* Black colleges in the South grew in size and stature with the expansion of graduate degree studies.
* Libraries throughout the rural South provided access to books for thousands of blacks and whites.
* Teacher-training programs at Southern colleges prepared men and women professionally for careers in rural classrooms.
* Access to medical clinics and hospitals improved the lives of millions in the South.
* Fellowships allowed hundreds of qualified black men and women to pursue careers as college presidents and professors, writers, and musicians.

But it was the Rosenwald School Building Program that directly affected *more* people. From 1912 to 1932, Julius Rosenwald and his fund were responsible for the building of 5,357 schools for black children in fifteen Southern states.

With the passage of the Civil Rights Act of 1964, school segregation officially ended. By law, black and white students could now attend school together. Many of the Rosenwald schools were closed or remodeled. Some were turned into private homes, community centers, or senior citizen centers, but a number of the original school buildings were abandoned and fell into ruin. When the

Built in 1921, the Columbia Rosenwald School, East Columbia, Texas, closed in 1948. The building was abandoned and fell into disrepair. With a grant from the National Trust for Historic Preservation, the building was moved, restored, and reopened in 2009 as a museum.

In 2010, several dozen billionaires, led by Microsoft cofounder Bill Gates and investor Warren Buffett, signed a "Giving Pledge," donating half of their fortunes to charities. Although they did not require matching funds from recipients, they still followed Julius Rosenwald's example of doing good with their wealth during their lifetimes.

Rosenwald school in Acworth, Georgia, was to be torn down to make way for a new building, residents "wanted to keep it. So they took the building apart, board by board, nail by nail, and moved it two blocks away."

But even as the original buildings disappeared or were neglected, memories of these schools have remained. Rosenwald school alumni across the South have erected historical markers or plaques at the schools or at their former locations.

In Columbus, Georgia, outside a modern brick school building, a roadside plaque tells passersby, "William H. Spencer High School. On this site, on November 29, 1930, the first local high school for colored students opened. The school was the result of a grant from the Rosenwald Foundation." A Florida state historical marker at the site of the Milner-Rosenwald Academy in Mount Dora reads in part: "Despite the inequity of segregation,

Milner-Rosenwald was a source of community pride. Its graduates were leaders, scholars, writers and contributing members of society."

Rosenwald graduates and their families also hold reunions. At one, more than a hundred alumni came. A graduate commented, "When I said I was going to my elementary school reunion, my friends laughed. They'd never heard of having an elementary school reunion." Alumni of the Rosenwald School in Waynesboro, Virginia, get together every three years to reminisce. "Everyone who went to school is like family," recalled Buddy Stewart, the president of the Rosenwald Reunion Committee. Another former student said, "As long as you have somebody to tell about it, the history won't be lost." Yet another remembered, "Your creativity was encouraged. You could express yourself and be yourself. . . . In an era of Jim Crow and segregation, I feel I got a good education."

"We were just fortunate to have people in the community who wanted to see us get an education."

The Scrabble School in Rappahannock County, Virginia, a Rosenwald school, opened in 1921. It was rehabilitated and reopened in 2009 as the Rappahannock Senior Center at Scrabble School with support from the National Trust for Historic Preservation.

At a reunion of the Toney Rosenwald School in Toney, Alabama, a graduate recalled, "Without the school, we'd have been whatever the white man wanted us to be. We didn't think we should be without buses and education. We wanted to have what everybody else in the country had at any cost." A second classmate added, "Things were changing fast, and they [community members] saw you needed to do more than plow and have crops." And another former student said, "So education was it."

Today, there is a growing interest in preserving the remaining five hundred or so Rosenwald schools throughout the South and keeping alive the memories of those schools that no longer exist. In 2002, the National Trust for Historic Preservation put the Rosenwald schools of the South on its list of most endangered historic sites in America. Through the trust's Rosenwald Initiative and local preservation groups, people are encouraged to support the restoration or recycling of the remaining Rosenwald school buildings.

Former students and their children and grandchildren are also taking action. When Wilbert Dean saw that his old school in Dillwyn, Virginia, was about to become a trash dump, he knew he had to save it. "Without this school," he said, "I would not be standing here today, because the school gave me an opportunity to finish high school." The National Trust for Historic Preservation, with help from other alumni, remodeled this former Rosenwald school into a community center.

In some places, volunteers are interviewing the oldest Rosenwald school graduates and recording their personal experiences. Their stories will help future generations understand how Rosenwald schools changed people's lives. A newspaper reporter wrote about the schools: "Even if many of the buildings are gone, what went on inside lives on in the memories of generations of black residents. They [former students] talk of fetching wood for the stoves, using outdoor privies and, most of all, learning from loving teachers." One of the former students he interviewed said, "We were just fortunate to have people in the community who wanted to see us get an education."

For more than six hundred thousand African American children, the Rosenwald schools offered hope and an escape from poverty at a time of extreme discrimination and segregation. Even when the building program ended in the early 1930s, the existing Rosenwald schools continued to provide education to children for decades. Charles Morgan Jr., a noted civil rights lawyer, reflected on the role played by Rosenwald school graduates in the fight for equality: "From those schools came the parents of the generation who marched and sang and risked their lives in the revolution for equal justice under the law."

I am indebted to the following for making this book possible: Dr. Peter Ascoli, grandson of Julius Rosenwald and the author of *Julius Rosenwald*, for writing the foreword of this book and for reviewing the manuscript; Dr. Daryl Michael Scott, professor of history at Howard University, for his insightful review of this book; and my friend, the late writer Jim Haskins, for his encouragement; for research assistance and advice: Tracy Hayes, project manager, Rosenwald Schools Initiative of the National Trust for Historic Preservation; Dr. Mary Hoffschwelle, author of *The Rosenwald Schools of the American South*; Beth Howse, special collections librarian, the John Hope and Aurelia E. Franklin Library, Fisk University; Earl L. Ijames, curator, North Carolina Museum of History; Claudia Stack, Under the Kudzu (underthekudzu.org); Teena Maenza, editor, *Brazoria County News*, East Columbia, Texas; Dr. Juanita Johnson, former principal, Trenton Rosenwald Middle School, Trenton, Tennessee; and Harvey Sukenic, director, Hebrew College Library; thanks to Carolyn P. Yoder, my editor extraordinaire, for wise counsel and encouragement; and, as always, my wife, Rosalind, for her patience, keen eye, and support.

—*NHF*

The source of each quotation in this book is found below. The citation indicates the first words of the quotation and its document source. Almost all the sources are listed in the bibliography. Complete citations are provided for those sources not in the bibliography.

Foreword (page 6)

"How does it feel . . .": Ascoli, p. 173.

Chapter 1 (page 10)

"came to the aid . . .": Bullock, p. 139.

"When I stood up to sing . . .": Finkelstein, p. 107.

"We don't take coloreds.": Alex Ross, "Voice of the Century," *The New Yorker*, April 13, 2009, p. 78.

"most influential philanthropic force . . .": Bullock, p. 139.

"Tobacco keeps them . . .": Library of Congress, Prints and Photographs Division, loc.gov/pictures/resource/nclc.00525.

"Rural schools of all types . . .": Willis D. Weatherford, p. 120, books.google.com.

"The negro school-houses . . .": W. K. Tate, quoted in "Forty-Third Annual Report, State Superintendent of Education of South Carolina," p. 115, same as above.

Chapter 2 (page 18)

"mother, as a wife . . .": *Plattsburgh* (NY) *Daily Press*, September 15, 1936, p. 8.

"Fortune smiled on me . . .": Julius Rosenwald, "The Burden of Wealth," *The Saturday Evening Post*, January 5, 1929, pp. 12–13, quoted in Barbara H. Davis and Susan Fieldwaite, "The Long Term Effects of Public School/State University Induction Program," *The Professional Educator* 28, no. 2 (Fall 2006), p. 25.

"The aim of my life . . .": Werner, p. 30.

"satisfaction guaranteed . . .": "Julius Rosenwald (1862–1932)," Sears Archives, searsarchives.com/people/juliusrosenwald.htm.

"Never once in all that time . . .": Ascoli, p. 53.

"civilization is a method . . .": hullhouse.org/aboutus/history/html (site discontinued).

"to put Christian principles . . .": YMCA, ymca.net/about-us.

"It startled me . . .": "Give at Home, Says Jew," *New York Tribune*, June 16, 1913, p. 4.

"It is glorious . . .": Ascoli, p. 79.

"I had no schooling . . .": Washington, Project Gutenberg, gutenberg.org/catalog/world/readfile?fk_files=3274916.

"From the time that I can remember . . .": same as above.

"At Hampton, for the first time . . .": same as above.

*Websites active at time of publication

Chapter 3 (page 26)

"Julius Rosenwald was . . .": Diane Granat, "Saving the Rosenwald Schools," Alicia Patterson Foundation, aliciapatterson.org.

"In the first place . . .": Werner, p. viii.

"He is helping his own race . . .": Ascoli, p. 87.

"I belong to a people . . .": Werner, p. 122.

"I don't believe . . .": Tamara Mann, "Julius Rosenwald. One Man's Philanthropic Legacy," My Jewish Learning, myjewishlearning.com.

"are as bad . . .": Diane Granat, "Julius Rosenwald's Legacy," *Atlanta Jewish Times*, October 4, 2002, p. 28, atljewishtimes.com/archives/2002/100402cs.htm (page discontinued).

"It is almost always easier . . .": Edwin Kiester, Jr., "Giving Money Away Wisely Ought to Be a Piece of Cake," *Smithsonian*, March 1996.

"The people showed in a very acceptable . . .": Deutsch, p. 125.

Chapter 4 (page 32)

"tremendously interesting.": Ascoli, p. 139.

"Those who are happiest . . .": Washington, unpaged.

"expressed his appreciation . . .": Ascoli, p. 146.

"for the well-being . . .": Embree and Waxman, p. 28.

"Having made money . . .": "His Life Philosophy Told in a Few Words," *New York Times*, January 7, 1932.

"Negro children may be . . .": "Education: Rosenwald Results," *Time*, December 11, 1933, time.com/time/magazine/article/0,9171,746525,00.html.

"I would rather be . . .": Library of Congress, Chronicling America, chroniclingamerica.loc.gov/lccn/sn83030214/1922-01-14/ed-1/seg-9/ (page discontinued).

"care should be taken . . .": "Lighting the Classroom," *Community School Plans*, Nashville, TN: Julius Rosenwald Fund, 1924, rosenwaldplans.org.

"well-trained Negro . . .": Smith, p. 65.

"as not to injure the eyes . . .": "General Directions for Painting Community Schools," *Community School Plans*, Nashville, TN: Julius Rosenwald Fund, 1924, rosenwaldplans.org.

"provide only formal and theoretical . . .": Embree and Waxman, p. 39.

"improved sanitation for better health . . .": Hoffschwelle, *Preserving Rosenwald Schools*, p. 7.

"Make walks wide enough . . .": "Suggestions for Beautifying School Grounds," *Community Schools Plans*, leaflet no. 2, July 1923, rosenwaldplans.org.

Chapter 5 (page 44)

"Considering all the things . . .": Reed, p. 85.

"Financial Educational Rally," "prominent visitors," "free dinner served," and "Realizing the fact . . .": Finkelstein, p. 92.

"they saved by eating . . .": Embree and Waxman, p. 49.

"so that his . . .": same as above, p. 50.

"We gave parties . . .": Mabel Orman Heard, interviewed on May 16, 1979, Institute for Oral History, Baylor University, baylor.edu/lib/index.php?id=76025&_buref=447-75995.

"children without shoes . . .": Anderson, p. 162.

"colored men offered . . .": same as above.

"men who worked . . .": same as above.

"sponsored socials and taffy pulls . . .": Walker, p. 17.

"men went to the woods . . .": same as above, p. 165.

"Within a month . . .": Embree and Waxman, p. 45.

"be set aside in . . .": Sosland, p. 44.

"that people in each school . . .": same as above.

"Textbooks should be . . .": Phyllis McClure, "Rosenwald Schools in the Northern Neck," *Virginia Magazine of History and Biography*, vol. 113, no. 2, p. 138.

Chapter 6 (page 52)

"When this building . . .": Dr. Penny Perry, quoted in Natalie Bullock-Brown, "Rosenwald Schools Discovered," UNC-TV, unctv.org/ncnow/storycopy.html.

"At least if you . . .": Erik Eckholm, "Black Schools Restored as Landmarks," *New York Times*, January 15, 2010, p. A16, nytimes.com/2010/01/15/us/15schools.htm.

"You could never finish . . .": Claudia Stack, "Symbols of Sacrifice," *Star-News* (Wilmington, NC), October 12, 2008, starnewsonline.com.

"In the mornings . . .": "No Easy Journey: Understanding Our Struggle for Justice and Education," *Daily Press* (Newport News, VA), May 1, 2004, p. 4, dailypress.com.

"She had boys in there . . .": Verdell Williams, quoted in Larry Copeland, "Partnership to Preserve Places of Black Opportunity," *USA Today*, April 6, 2008, usatoday30.usatoday.com/news/education/2008-04-06-oldschools_N.htm.

"If the teachers told . . .": Merlene Davis, "Great Expectations," *Lexington* (KY) *Herald-Leader*, July 16, 2006.

"The teacher would send . . .": Samuel McDonald, Jr., "Rosenwald School Oral History Excerpts," Robeson County (NC) Schools Oral History Project.

"There were a lot of . . .": Mary Openshaw, "Preserving the Past," *The Facts* (Brazoria County, TX), October 21, 2009, thefacts.com.

"one-fourth of all . . . ": Anderson, p. 179.

"the Fund provided . . .": Sosland, p. 43.

"The Rosenwald training . . .": "Black History: A Memory Reborn," *Houston Chronicle*, October 24, 2009.

"The purpose of formal education . . .": Perkins, p. 126.

"My own guess is . . .": Ascoli, p. 371.

"over 12,000 library sets . . .": Embree and Waxman, p. 61.

"Who's Who of black America . . .": Adams and Bracey, p. 5.

"No race or class . . .": *New York Times*, January 11, 1941.

"feeling of inferiority . . .": "Teaching with Documents: Order of Argument in the Case, *Brown v. Board of Education*," National Archives, U.S. National Archives and Records Administration, archives.gov/education/lessons/brown-case-order/.

Chapter 7 (page 62)

"What I want to do is . . .": Werner, p. viii.

"One of his most conspicuous . . .": "Hoover Mourns Passing," *New York Times*, January 7, 1932.

"Julius Rosenwald used . . .": Werner, p. 355.

"the death of Julius Rosenwald . . .": W. E. B. Du Bois, in *Crisis*, February 1932, p. 58, as quoted in Ascoli, p. 385.

"such educational, benevolent . . .": Alicia S. Roberts, "Rosenwald, Julius," Learning to Give, Center on Philanthropy at Indiana University, learningtogive.org/papers/paper121.html.

"All the Fund's work was in faith . . .": Embree and Waxman, p. 209.

"Giving Pledge": The Giving Pledge, givingpledge.org.

"Without the Rosenwald Fund . . .": Joe Levine, "Bond. George Bond," TC Media Center, Teachers College, Columbia University, May 13, 2009, tc.columbia.edu/news/article.htm?id=6992.

"wanted to keep it . . .": Larry Copeland, "Partnership to Preserve Places of Black Opportunity," *USA Today*, April 7, 2008, usatoday30. usatoday.com/news/education/2008-04-06-oldschools_N.htm.

"William H. Spencer High School . . .": Historic Markers Across Georgia, Latitude 34 North, lat34north.com/historicmarkers/LargePhoto.cfm?keyId=106-A60&PicSuffix=&MarkerTitle=William%20H.%20Spencer%20High%20School.

"Despite the inequity . . .": Sara F. Luther, *Schooldays at Milner-Rosenwald*, Eschar Publications, 2008, p. 7.

"When I said . . .": Morehouse Economic Development Corporation, morehouseedc.org/news/2005/rosenwald.htm (site discontinued).

"Everyone who went . . .": Tony Gonzalez, "Rosenwald Reunion," *News Virginian* (Waynesboro, VA), February 20, 2010.

"As long as you . . .": same as above.

"Your creativity was encouraged . . .": same as above.

"Without the school . . .": Mike Marshall, "The Toney Rosenwald School: 'We Will Not Forget,'" *Huntsville* (AL) *Times*, AL.com, blog.al.com/breaking/2010/09/the_toney_ rosenwald_school_we.html.

"Things were changing . . .": same as above.

"So education was it.": same as above.

"Without this school . . .": Susan Logue Koster, "US Segregation-Era Schools Get New Life," Voice of America, February 25, 2010, voanews.com/english/news/education/ loguerosenwaldschools25feb10-85379212.html.

"Even if many of the buildings . . .": Joey Holleman, "Rosenwald Schools Face Extinction," *State* (Columbia, SC), June 11, 2007, find.galegroup.com.ezproxy.bpl.org/gtx/start. do?prodId=GRGM.

"We were just fortunate . . .": same as above.

"From those schools . . .": Sosland, unpaged.

Books

Adams, Maurianne, and John H. Bracey, eds. *Strangers and Neighbors: Relations between Blacks and Jews in the United States.* Amherst: University of Massachusetts Press, 2000.

Anderson, James D. *The Education of Blacks in the South, 1860–1935.* Chapel Hill: University of North Carolina Press, 1988.

Ascoli, Peter M. *Julius Rosenwald: The Man Who Built Sears, Roebuck and Advanced the Cause of Black Education in the American South.* Bloomington: Indiana University Press, 2006.

Bullock, Henry Allen. *A History of Negro Education in the South: From 1619 to the Present.* Cambridge, MA: Harvard University Press, 1967.

Davis, John P., ed. *The American Negro Reference Book.* Englewood Cliffs, NJ: Prentice-Hall, 1966.

Deutsch, Stephanie. *You Need a Schoolhouse: Booker T. Washington, Julius Rosenwald, and the Building of Schools for the Segregated South.* Evanston, IL: Northwestern University Press, 2011.

Embree, Edwin R. *Julius Rosenwald Fund: Review of Two Decades, 1917–1936.* Chicago: Julius Rosenwald Fund, 1936.

Embree, Edwin R., and Julia Waxman. *Investment in People: The Story of the Julius Rosenwald Fund.* New York: Harper and Brothers, 1949.

Finkelstein, Norman H. *Heeding the Call: Jewish Voices in America's Civil Rights Struggle.* Philadelphia: Jewish Publication Society, 1997.

Foner, Eric. *Forever Free: The Story of Emancipation and Reconstruction.* New York: Alfred Knopf, 2005.

Hart, Albert Bushnell. *The Southern South.* New York: D. Appleton, 1912.

Hoffschwelle, Mary S. *Preserving Rosenwald Schools.* Washington, DC: National Trust for Historic Preservation, 2003.

———. *The Rosenwald Schools of the American South.* Gainesville: University Press of Florida, 2006.

Perkins, Alfred. *Edward Rogers Embree: The Julius Rosenwald Fund, Foundation Philanthropy, and American Race Relations.* Bloomington: Indiana University Press, 2011.

Reed, Betty Jamerson. *The Brevard Rosenwald School: Black Education and Community Building in a Southern Appalachian Town, 1920–1926.* Jefferson, NC: McFarland, 2004.

Smith, S. L. *Builders of Goodwill: The Story of the State Agents of Negro Education in the South, 1910 to 1950*. Nashville: Tennessee Book Company, 1950.

Sosland, Jeffrey K. *A School in Every County: The Partnership of Jewish Philanthropist Julius Rosenwald and American Black Communities*. Washington, DC: Economics and Science Planning, 1995.

Walker, Vanessa Siddle. *Their Highest Potential: An African American School Community in the Segregated South*. Chapel Hill: University of North Carolina Press, 1996.

Washington, Booker T. *Up from Slavery: An Autobiography*. Garden City, NY: Doubleday, 1963.

Weatherford, Carole Boston. *Dear Mr. Rosenwald*. New York: Scholastic Press, 2006.

Weatherford, Willis D. *Present Forces in Negro Progress*. New York: Association Press, 1912.

Werner, M. R. *Julius Rosenwald: The Life of a Practical Humanitarian*. New York: Harper and Brothers, 1939.

The following journals and newspapers are cited in the Source Notes:

Daily Press (Newport News, VA)
Houston Chronicle
Huntsville (AL) *Times*
Lexington (KY) *Herald-Leader*
News Virginian (Waynesboro, VA)
The New Yorker
New York Times
New York Tribune
Plattsburgh (NY) *Daily Press*
The Professional Educator
Saturday Evening Post
Smithsonian magazine
Star-News (Wilmington, NC)
State (Columbia, SC)
Time magazine
USA Today
Virginia Magazine of History and Biography

Websites*

AL.com, Huntsville. al.com/huntsville

Alicia Patterson Foundation. aliciapatterson.org

Atlanta Jewish Times. atljewishtimes.com

Charlotte-Mecklenburg Historic Landmarks Commission.
    cmhpf.org/index.html

The Facts (Brazoria County, TX). thefacts.com

History South. historysouth.org/rosenwaldhome.html

Hull House. hullhouse.org/aboutus/history/html
    (site discontinued)

Institute for Oral History, Baylor University. baylor.edu/lib

Latitude 34 North. lat34north.com

Learning to Give, Center on Philanthropy at Indiana University.
    learningtogive.org

Library of Congress, Chronicling America.
    chroniclingamerica.loc.gov

Library of Congress, Prints and Photographs
    Division. loc.gov/pictures

My Jewish Learning. myjewishlearning.com

National Archives, U.S. National Archives and Records
    Administration. archives.gov

Project Gutenberg. gutenberg.org

Sears Archives. searsarchives.com

Teachers College, Columbia University. tc.columbia.edu

UNC-TV. unctv.org

Voice of America. voanews.com/english/news/education/
    loguerosenwaldschools25feb10-85379212.html

Young Men's Christian Association (YMCA). ymca.net

Websites active at time of publication

77

INDEX

Page numbers in **boldface** refer to images and/or captions.

PICTURE CREDITS

Courtesy of Peter Ascoli: 18.

Fisk University Franklin Library's Special Collections: 270: 44; 3067: 48; 1393: 49.

The Image Works: ERVL0327005: 62.

Library of Congress, Prints and Photographs Division: LC-DIG-nclc-00519: 1, 16–17; LC-DIG-ggbain-22613: 6; LC-DIG-ppmsca-19253: 14; LC-USZ62-117666: 15; LC-USZ62-94702: 20; LC-DIG-ppmsca-13307: 23; LC-B8171-152-A: 24; LC-USZ62-2248: 25; LC-USZ62-78481: 31; LC-USZ62-134343: 41; LC-USZ62-75055: 51; LC-USZ62-11573: 61; LC-USZ62-111719: 64; Harris & Ewing Collection, LC-DIG-hec-08365: front jacket flap; Visual Materials from the NAACP Records, LC-DIG-ppmsca-23838: 10; NYWT&S Collection, LC-USZ62-129809: 13 (right).

Teena Maenza: 65 (top).

Museum of Science and Industry, Chicago, Joe Ziolkowski: 28 (right).

National Trust for Historic Preservation: 9, 67.

Scurlock Studio Records, Archives Center, National Museum of American History, Behring Center, Smithsonian Institution: 12.

Tennessee State Library and Archives: 2252: 13 (left); 10#6272: 54.

University of Chicago Libraries, Department of Special Collections: 7, 26, 28 (left), 29, 34, 36, 43, 56, 57, 65 (bottom); Rosenwald Papers, Box 39, Folder 24: 32, 35; Rosenwald Scrapbook #5: 50.

University of Virginia Library, Special Collections, Jackson Davis Papers: 2001: front jacket, 2–3, 37 (top right); 2362: 4; 2585: 4–5; 1611: 37 (top left); L1177: 37 (bottom); 1610: 38; 1611: 39; L1167: 42; 6158: 46; 2510: 52; 2371: 59, back jacket.